Sing 'n Learn™
KOREAN
노래하며 배우는 한국어
Introduce Korean with Favorite Children's Songs

By Bo-Kyung Kim and Selina Yoon
Concept and Design by Selina Yoon
Music arrangement by Rob Currens
Illustrations by Animation Ink, Inc.
Voice by Esther Hyun

MASTER
COMMUNICATIONS

Published by Master Communications, P.O. Box 9096, Cincinnati, Ohio 45209-0096 U.S.A.
© 1997 Master Communications, Inc. All rights reserved. No part of this book may be reproduced, stored, in a retrieval system, or transmitted in any form or by any means, electronic, mechanical, photocopying, recording or otherwise, without the prior permission of Master Communications.

Printed in the United States of America.
ISBN 1-888194-08-1

The Korean language belongs to the "Altaic" language group. The written Korean system, Hangul, was created in 1443 by King Sejong and his scholars. Hangul was created on the basis of a scientific linguistic analysis. For example, the consonants were given the cross-section outline based upon the appearance of the way the tongue move to articulate the sound.

Korean grammar is very different from that of English. Korean word order within a sentence structure is quite different. In Korean, the word order is subject-object-verb compared to the order of subject-verb-object in English.

In this book, we have chosen to use Hangul for the lyrics without the romanization as the current romanization system is quite complex and Hangul is relatively easy to pick-up.

The Korean Letters and Their Sounds

There are 14 basic consonants and 10 basic vowels. In addition, there are five double consonants and 11 combined vowels.

Consonant Letters

ㄱ g,k as in "go"
ㄴ n as in "name"
ㄷ d,t as in "do" or "tow"
ㄹ r or l as in "red" or "little"
ㅁ m in "milk"
ㅂ b as in "boy"
ㅅ s as in "sleep" and "speech"
ㅇ -ng as in "sing" or "ah"
ㅈ j as in "joy"
ㅊ ch as in "chair"
ㅋ k as in "kind"
ㅌ t as in "tide"
ㅍ p as in "pie"
ㅎ h as in "hat"

ㄲ k as in "sky"
ㄸ t as in "stay"
ㅃ p as in "apple"
ㅆ s as in "sell" or "essential"
ㅉ ts as in "sports"

Vowel Letters

ㅏ a as in "father"
ㅑ ya as in "yarn"
ㅓ u as in "hut"
ㅕ you as in "young"
ㅗ o as in "oh"
ㅛ yo as in "yoke"
ㅜ oo or u as in "mood" or "do"
ㅠ u or you as in "useful" or "youth"
ㅡ e as in "taken"
ㅣ i as in "ink"

ㅐ a as in "sat"
ㅒ ya as in "yam"
ㅔ e as in "set"
ㅖ ye as in "yes"
ㅚ Close to the eu in the French "peur"
ㅘ wa as in "wand"
ㅙ wa as in "wag"
ㅟ we or wie as in "We" or "wield"
ㅝ wo as in "won"
ㅞ we as in "wet"
ㅢ Between the wie of "wield" and I of "machine"

Consonants and vowels are grouped into syllabic clusters to form words. Hangul, 한글, for example is made of combination of consonants and vowels from left to right and top to bottom.

ㅎ(h) ㅏ(a) ㄴ(n) and ㄱ(g) ㅡ(u) ㄹ(l)

When there are no initial consonants, it is replaced by ㅇ as in 아(a)

Below are examples of words from the lyrics:

See page 32 for more examples.

안녕 (an-nyung) hello or good-bye
친구 (chin-gu) friend

하나 (ha-na) one
둘 (dul or dool) two
셋 (set) three
넷 (net) four
다섯 (da-suht) five
여섯 (yo-suht) six
일곱 (il-gop) seven
여덟 (yo-dol) eight
아홉 (ah-hope) nine
열 (yol) ten

머리 (muh-ry) head, hair
눈 (noon) eyes, snow
귀 (kwi) ear
코 (ko) nose
입 (ip) mouth
손 (sohn) hand
어깨 (uh-kke) shoulder
무릎 (mu-rup) knee
발 (bahl) foot
다리 (dah-ri) leg, bridge
학교 (hahk-kyo) school
선생님 (son-saeng-nim) teacher
비행기 (bi-haeng-ki) airplane

Hello

안녕

안녕 잘 있었니
반가워 안녕
함께 노래하며
재미있는 시간
가지자 안녕

타미 **Tommy Panda**

페니 **Penny Panda**

3

Ten Friends

열 친구

한 친구 두 친구
세 친구 모여
네 친구 다섯 친구
여섯 친구 모여
일곱 친구 여덟 친구
아홉 친구 모여
열 친구 모였네

School

학교

학교 종이 땡땡땡 어서 모이자
선생님이 우리를 기다리신다

5

Early in the Morning

아침 일찍

얼굴은 이렇게 세수를 하세요 하세요
이렇게 세수를 하세요 아침 일찍

이를 이렇게 닦아요 닦아요 닦아요
이를 깨끗이 닦아요 아침 일찍

머리를 이렇게 빗어요 빗어요 빗어요
머리를 예쁘게 빗어요 아침 일찍

옷을 이렇게 입어요 입어요 입어요
옷을 예쁘게 입어요 아침 일찍

세수를 해요

이를 닦아요

머리를 빗어요

옷을 입어요

Friends

친구들아

우리 친구들 모여라 모여라 모여라
우리 친구들 만날 때는 더 즐겁다
너의 친구는 나의 친구
나의 친구는 너의 친구
우리 친구들 만날 때는 더 즐겁다

우리 친구들 모여라 모여라 모여라
우리 친구들과 놀 때는 더 즐겁다
너의 친구는 나의 친구
나의 친구는 너의 친구
우리 친구들과 놀 때는 더 즐겁다

손뼉

만세

발 굴려

Let's All Happily...

모두 즐겁게

우리 모두 즐겁게 손뼉을 (짝짝)
우리 모두 즐겁게 손뼉을 (짝짝)
우리 모두 즐겁게 기쁜 노래부르며
우리 모두 즐겁게 손뼉을 (짝짝)

우리 모두 즐겁게 발 굴려 (쾅쾅)
우리 모두 즐겁게 발 굴려 (쾅쾅)
우리 모두 즐겁게 기쁜 노래부르며
우리 모두 즐겁게 발 굴려 (쾅쾅)

우리 모두 즐겁게 만세해 (만세)
우리 모두 즐겁게 만세해 (만세)
우리 모두 즐겁게 기쁜 노래부르며
우리 모두 즐겁게 만세해 (만세)

우리 모두 즐겁게 전부다 (짝짝 쾅쾅 만세)
우리 모두 즐겁게 전부다 (짝짝 쾅쾅 만세)
우리 모두 즐겁게 기쁜 노래부르며
우리 모두 즐겁게 전부다 (짝짝 쾅쾅 만세)

Airplane

비행기

떴다 떴다 비행기
날아라 날아라
우리 우리 비행기
높이 날아라

Puppy

강아지

우리집 강아지는 복슬 강아지
어머니가 빨래가면 멍멍멍
쫄랑쫄랑 따라가며 멍멍멍

우리집 강아지는 예쁜 강아지
학교 갔다 돌아오면 멍멍멍
꼬리치며 반갑다고 멍멍멍

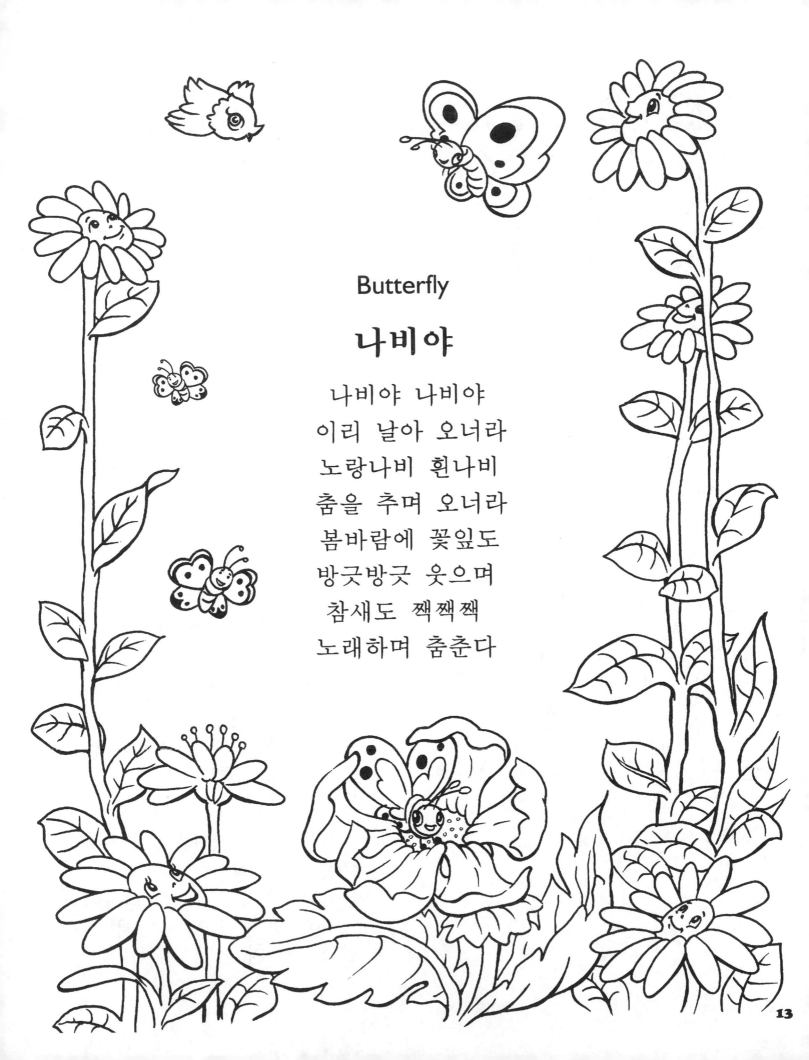

Butterfly

나비야

나비야 나비야
이리 날아 오너라
노랑나비 흰나비
춤을 추며 오너라
봄바람에 꽃잎도
방긋방긋 웃으며
참새도 짹짹짹
노래하며 춤춘다

Hokey Pokey
호키포키

다 같이 오른손을 안에 넣고
오른손을 밖에 빼고
오른손을 안에 넣고 힘껏 흔들어
호키포키 하며 빙빙 돌면서
즐겁게 춤추자

다 같이 왼손을 안에 넣고
왼손을 밖에 빼고
왼손을 안에 넣고 힘껏 흔들어
호키포키 하며 빙빙 돌면서
즐겁게 춤추자

다 같이 오른발을 안에 넣고
오른발을 밖에 빼고
오른발을 안에 넣고 힘껏 흔들어
호키포키 하며 빙빙 돌면서
즐겁게 춤추자

다 같이 왼발을 안에 넣고
왼발을 밖에 빼고
왼발을 안에 넣고 힘껏 흔들어
호키포키 하며 빙빙 돌면서
즐겁게 춤추자

다 같이 온몸을 안에 넣고
온몸을 밖에 빼고
온몸을 안에 넣고 힘껏 흔들어
호키포키 하며 빙빙 돌면서
즐겁게 춤추자

무릎

어깨

머리

발

Head, Shoulders, Knees & Feet

머리 어깨 무릎 발

머리 어깨 무릎 발 무릎 발
머리 어깨 무릎 발 무릎 발
눈 귀 입과 코
머리 어깨 무릎 발 무릎 발

눈

귀

입

코

귀는 둘

눈도 둘

코는 하나

Two Ears

귀는 둘

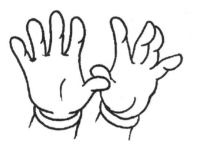

손가락은 열

귀는 둘이요 눈도 둘이요
코는 하나 입도 하나요
머리는 하나 손은 둘이요
발도 둘이요 손가락은 열
라라라라라 라라라라라
라라라라라 라라라라라

입도 하나

발도 둘

손은 둘

머리는 하나

Where is ...?

어디 있나

하나 둘 셋 넷
다섯 여섯 일곱
우리 친구 어디 있나
여기 있네 여기 있네
우리 친구 여기 있네

하나 둘 셋 넷
다섯 여섯 일곱
우리 동생 어디 있나
여기 있네 여기 있네
우리 동생 여기 있네

3) 오빠　　4) 언니

1	2	3	4	5	6	7	8	9	10
하나	둘	셋	넷	다섯	여섯	일곱	여덟	아홉	열

What Color?

무슨 색깔

빨간 빨간색
누가 입었나
빨간 빨간 빨간색
타미가 입었네

보라 보라색
누가 입었나
보라 보라 보라색
페니가 입었네

Uncle had a Farm Field
아저씨는 밭 있어

아저씨는 밭 있어 이야이야오
그 밭에 오리 있거든 이야이야오
여기 꽥꽥꽥 저기 꽥꽥꽥
여기 꽥 저기 꽥 여기저기 꽥꽥
아저씨는 밭 있어 이야이야오

아저씨는 밭 있어 이야이야오
그 밭에 강아지 있거든 이야이야오
여기 멍멍멍 저기 멍멍멍
여기 멍 저기 멍 여기저기 멍멍
아저씨는 밭 있어 이야이야오

아저씨는 밭 있어 이야이야오
그 밭에 고양이 있거든 이야이야오
여기 야옹 야옹 야옹
저기 야옹 야옹 야옹
여기 야옹 저기 야옹
여기저기 야옹 야옹
아저씨는 밭 있어 이야이야오

아저씨는 밭 있어 이야이야오
그 밭에 돼지 있거든 이야이야오
여기 꿀꿀꿀 저기 꿀꿀꿀
여기 꿀 저기 꿀 여기저기 꿀꿀
아저씨는 밭 있어 이야이야오

Five Little Ducks

다섯 마리 새끼오리

다섯 마리 새끼오리 놀러나가
언덕을 넘어 멀리 가
엄마 오리가 꽥꽥꽥
네 마리 오리만 달려와

네 마리 새끼 오리 놀러나가
언덕을 넘어 멀리 가
엄마 오리가 꽥꽥꽥
세 마리 오리만 달려와

세 마리 새끼 오리 놀러나가
언덕을 넘어 멀리 가
엄마 오리가 꽥꽥꽥
두 마리 오리만 달려와

두 마리 새끼오리 놀러나가
언덕을 넘어 멀리 가
엄마 오리가 꽥꽥꽥
한 마리 오리만 달려와

한 마리 새끼오리 놀러나가
언덕을 넘어 멀리 가
엄마 오리가 꽥꽥꽥
아무 오리도 오지 않아

그래서 엄마 오리가 여기저기 찾다가
아주 큰소리로 꽥꽥꽥 불렀더니

다섯 마리 오리 모두 달려와

London Bridge

런던다리

런던다리 무너져 무너져 무너져
런던다리 무너져 다리가 무너져

Words Ending with "Ri"

리리리자로

리리리자로 끝나는 말은
개구리 병아리 코끼리
도토리 유리 항아리

Snow

눈

펄-펄 눈이 옵니다
바람 타고 눈이 옵니다
하늘나라 선녀님들이
송이송이 하얀솜을
자꾸자꾸 뿌려줍니다
자꾸자꾸 뿌려줍니다

Thunder
천둥

천둥이 꽝꽝
번개가 번쩍
꽝꽝꽝 번쩍
소나기가 온다
좍 좍 좍
푹 젖었네
푹 젖었네

Rain
비

비야 멈춰라
다른 날에 오너라
밖에 나가 놀게
비야 비야 멈춰라

26

Twinkle, Twinkle, Little Star

작은 별

반짝 반짝 작은 별
아름답게 비치네
동쪽 하늘에서도
서쪽 하늘에서도
반짝반짝 작은 별
아름답게 비치네

27

Good-bye Song

인사노래

헤어지면 언제 만나
새달에 새해에
아니아니 내일
바로바로 내일
만나자 안녕

28

1. Hello *Page 3*

Hello, How are you? (informal form)
Glad to see you. Hello.
Let's sing together and
Have a fun time.
How are you?

2. Ten Friends *Page 4*

One friend, two friends, three friends together,
Four friends, five friends, six friends together,
Seven friends, eight friends, nine friends together,
Ten friends get together.

3. School *Page 5*

The school bells are ringing, ring ring ring,
Let's get together.
The teacher is waiting for us.

4. Early in the Morning *Page 6*

This is the way we wash our face,
wash our face, wash our face,
This is the way we wash our face,
Early in the morning.

This is the way we brush our teeth,
brush our teeth, brush our teeth,
We brush our teeth cleanly,
Early in the morning.

This is the way we comb our hair,
comb our hair, comb our hair,
We comb our hair well,
Early in the morning.

This is the way we put on our clothes,
put on our clothes, put on our clothes,
We put on our clothes well,
Early in the morning.

5. Friends *Page 8*

Let our friends get together, together, together.
When we get together, the happier we would be.
Your friend is my friend, my friend is your friend,
When we get together, the happier we would be.

Let our friends get together, together, together.
When we play together, the happier we would be.
Your friend is my friend, my friend is your friend,
When we play together, the happier we would be.

6. Let's All Happily *Page 10*

Let's all happily, clap our hands
Let's all happily, clap our hands
Let's all sing a happy song and
Let's all happily, clap our hands.

2) stomp your feet
3) shout hooray
4) all three (clap, stomp, hooray)

7. Airplane *Page 12*

The airplane, up in the air, up in the air.
Fly, fly.
Our airplane, fly up high in the air.

8. Puppy *Page 12*

Our puppy is a cute, furry puppy.
When mommy goes to wash clothes, mung mung mung
Follows her "mung mung mung".
Our puppy is a good puppy.
When I come back from school, greets me by wagging his
tail "mung mung mung."

9. Butterfly *Page 13*

Butterfly, butterfly, come fly this way,
Yellow butterfly, white butterfly dance this way.
The flowers are smiling in the spring breeze.
The birds are also singing, "chirp, chirp, chirp" and dancing.

10. Hokey Pokey *Page 14*

Everyone, put your right hand in, put your right hand out,
Put your right hand in, and shake your hand,
Do the hokey pokey, turn yourself around and dance merrily.

2) left hand
3) right foot
4) left foot
5) whole self in

11. Head, Shoulders, Knees & Feet *Page 16*

Head, shoulders, knees and feet, knees and feet
Head, shoulders, knees and feet, knees and feet
Eyes, ears, mouth and nose
Head, shoulders, knees and feet, knees and feet.

12. Two Ears *Page 17*

There are two ears, two eyes, one nose,
One mouth, one head, two hands
Two feet, ten fingers
La la la la la la la la la la
La la la la la la la la la la

1, 2, 3, 4, 5, 6, 7, 8, 9, 10 *Page 18*

13. Where is ? *Page 18*

One, two, three, four, five, six, seven
Where is my friend?
Here he is, here he is
Here is my friend!

One, two, three, four, five, six, seven
Where is my younger sister (brother)?
Here (s)he is, here (s)he is
Here is my younger sister (brother)!

3) older brother
4) older sister

14. What Color? *Page 19*

Red, red color,
Who's wearing red?
Red, red, red, red color
Tommy's wearing red.

Purple, purple color
Who's wearing purple?
Purple, purple, purple, purple color
Penny's wearing purple.

15. Uncle had a Farm Field *Page 20*

Uncle has a farm field, I EI I EI O
He raises ducks in the field, I EI I EI O
Here quack quack quack, there quack quack quack
here quack, there quack, here, there quack quack.
2) Puppy -- mung mung mung mung
3) Cat -- yaong, yaong, yaong
4) Pig -- kkul, kkul, kkul, kkul

16. Five Little Ducks *Page 22*

Five little ducks went out to play
Over the hills and far away,
Mommy duck said quack quack quack,
Four little ducks came running back.
Four little ducks went out to play
Over the hills and far away,
Mommy duck said quack quack quack,
Three little ducks came running back.
Three little ducks went out to play
Over the hills and far away,
Mommy duck said quack quack quack,
Two little ducks came running back.
Two little ducks went out to play
Over the hills and far away,

Mommy duck said quack quack quack,
One little duck came running back.
One little duck went out to play
Over the hills and far away,
Mommy duck said quack quack quack,
No ducks came back.
Then, Mommy duck looked around and
said loudly QUACK QUACK QUACK,
All five little ducks came running back.

17. London Bridge *Page 24*

London bridge is falling down,
Falling down, falling down.
London bridge is falling down.
The bridge is falling down.

18. Words Ending with "Ri" *Page 25*

The words that end in "ri" sounds are frog (kae-gu-ri), chicks (pyong-a-ri), elephant (ko-kki-ri), acorn (do-to-ri), glass vase (yu-ri hang-a-ri).

19. Snow *Page 25*

The big snow flakes are falling and falling.
The fairy in the sky is sprinkling the white cotton balls again and again, again and again.

20. Thunder *Page 26*

It is thundering, it is lightning,
Boom, boom, boom, flash.
It is pouring,
Pour, pour, pour.
I am soaked, I am soaked!

21. Rain *Page 26*

Rain, go away, come again another day.
So we can play outside, rain, rain go away.

22. Twinkle, Twinkle, Little Star *Page 27*

Twinkle, twinkle, little star,
The beautiful and bright little stars.
Up above the eastern sky and the western sky,
Twinkle, twinkle, little star,
The beautiful and bright little stars.

23. Good-bye *Page 28*

When will we see each other?
Next month? Next year?
No, no, tomorrow. Of course, tomorrow.
See you soon. Good-bye.

Good-Bye!

Note: The translations are not always literal

Introduction — Sing & Learn Korean introduces the language in the context of many familiar tunes so that children can focus on learning new words and concepts. The songs are specially chosen to cover important basic concepts such as family, numbers, colors, action verbs, body parts, animals, and friendship. Please note that the lyrics do not have any punctuation marks in Korean.

1. Hello *Page 3*

Have one child sing the beginning part of the song and the others do the second part.
Replace the word "sing" with any other action words such as dance or jump.

2. Ten Friends *Page 4*

Helps with counting.
Point at the illustration as you count friends.
Place paper dolls or flannel dolls one at a time as you count.

3. School *Page 5*

This song can be sung in the morning before school starts or at school.
This is a very popular song in Korea.

4. Early in the Morning *Page 6*

Substitute words with activities relating to children's lives by asking "What do you do early in the morning?".
Children could act out what they are singing.
The repetitive patterns in this song help children learn the song and practice the language easily.

5. Friends *Page 8*

Ask children how they feel to get together with friends. Are they happy, Is it fun?

6. Let's All Happily *Page 10*

This song enhances young children's listening skills by following the directions in the song.
Replace the movement with other actions.
Ask children what they would do when they are happy and sing out their answers.

7. Airplane *Page 12*

A great song to sing with paper-folding activities. Fold paper to make an airplane, Fly them and sing the song.
This is a very popular song in Korea.

8. Puppy *Page 12*

The dog's barking sound is "mung mung mung" in Korea.
In the old days, women washed clothes in streams or small brooks, away from their houses. This is a very popular song in Korea.

9. Butterfly *Page 13*

This is a very popular song in Korea.
Flap arms to mimic fluttering of butterfly wings and form beaks with both hands when singing the last verse with the birds singing.

10. Hokey Pokey *Page 14*

This great sing-and-play song helps children become familiar with body parts in Korean. Also teaches the concept of "in" and "out".
Follow the action of the words.

11. Head, Shoulders, Knees & Feet *Page 16*

This song is great for gross motor skill development.
Helps children with body parts in Korean.
Follow the song by pointing at the head, shoulders, knees & feet with both hands.
Point at the illustrations of the song to help children become familiar with the Korean Hangul.

12. Two Ears *Page 17*

Excellent for helping children remember the body parts and numbers in Korean.
Ask children to fill in the numbers. For example, the teacher or parent sings "ears" and children say "2".
Follow the song by pointing at the body parts with both hands. When it comes to the ten fingers, move all ten fingers. Clap hands as you sing "la, la, la ....".

1, 2, 3, 4, 5, 6, 7, 8, 9, 10 *Page 18*

Count various objects.

13. Where is ? *Page 18*

Practice learning family members by replacing "friend" with "daddy," "mommy," "brother," or "sister."
Replace "friend" with any other words to practice vocabulary.
You can play a hide-and-seek game with this song.

14. What Color? *Page 19*

This song helps children learn their colors in a meaningful way.
Ask children "Who wears _____ today?" before starting the song.
Older children can make a book by putting a photo or a drawing on each page to identify colors and each child's name.
For reinforcement of colors, use the cover of the book for the color of clothes and rainbows.

15. Uncle had a Farm Field *Page 20*

Uncle is a generic term to refer to a man in Korea as the names are not commonly used. In Korea, most farmers do not have large farms; they have fields. This song introduces animals and their sounds in Korean to children.
We have selected more common animals for children.
The cow's sound is "Ume" in Korean.

16. Five Little Ducks *Page 22*

This is a great song to sing in the tub with rubber ducks. You can also use flannel ducks or duck puppets made out of paper and glued to popsicle sticks. Another way is to put one duck puppet on each of the fingers with rubber bands to sing with children.
To learn to express their feelings, ask children how mommy duck would have felt when she could not find her little ducks.

17. London Bridge *Page 24*

Ask children why they think the bridge fell down and how to fix a bridge. This can increase children's logical thinking and problem solving skills.
Act out the song like the illustration. Two children can join hands and form an arch. The other children form a single line to pass under the bridge. When the bridge falls at the end of the song, the child who is under the bridge becomes one of the children holding hands to make the arch.

18. Words Ending with "Ri" *Page 25*

This is a good phonics song in Korean. Point at the pictures as the songs are sung. The words that end in "ri" sounds are frog (kae-gu-ri), chicks (pyong-a-ri), elephant (ko-kki-ri), acorn (do-to-ri), glass vase (yu-ri han-ga-ri). Another word from the book is ducks (oh-ri).

19. Snow *Page 25*

A popular song in Korea. You can teach about the seasons of the year and the weather.

20. Thunder *Page 26*

Ask children what the sound of thunder is like.
Put cupped hands next to the ears as the second verse is sung and move fingers to simulate rain as arms are lowered.

21. Rain *Page 26*

Use different children's names to become familiar with each other's name.
Ask children about what they can do on a rainy day.

22. Twinkle, Twinkle, Little Star *Page 27*

Use finger movement to simulate the twinkles.
Point at the eastern sky and point at the western sky.

23. Good-bye *Page 28*

The informal "good-bye" (an-nyung) is the same as "hello" in Korean.

Below are more Korean words with pronunciation guides.

See page 2 for more details.

돼지 (twae-ji) pig
나비 (na-bi) butterfly
오리 (oh-ri) duck
강아지 (kang-a-ji) puppy
고양이 (ko-yang-i) cat
병아리 (byung-a-ri) chicks
코끼리 (ko-kki-ri) elephant
개구리 (ke-gu-ri) frog

엄마 (om-ma) mom (informal)
아빠 (a-ppa) dad (informal)
언니 (on-nie) older sister
오빠 (oh-ppa) older brother
동생 (dong-seng) younger sister or brother

색깔 (saek-kkal) color
빨간색 (ppal-gan-saek) red color
보라색 (po-ra-saek) purple color
노란색 (no-ran-saek) yellow color
파란색 (pa-ran-saek) blue color
초록색 (cho-rok-saek) green color

눈 (noon) snow
바람 (bah-rahm) wind
번개 (buhn-gae) lightening
별 (byul) star
비 (bi) rain
소나기 (soh-na-gi) shower
천둥 (chon-dung) thunder